Bibliographic information published by the German National Library:

The German National Library lists this publication in the National Bibliography; detailed bibliographic data are available on the Internet at http://dnb.dnb.de .

Imprint:

Copyright © 2012 GRIN Verlag
Print and binding: Books on Demand GmbH, Norderstedt Germany
ISBN: 9783668905344

Aasha Ajith

How Can a Loss of Information in Mixed Attribute Datasets be Prevented?

On the Imputation of Missing Values in Mixed Attribute Datasets Using Higher Order Kernel Functions

GRIN Verlag

GRIN - Your knowledge has value

Since its foundation in 1998, GRIN has specialized in publishing academic texts by students, college teachers and other academics as e-book and printed book. The website www.grin.com is an ideal platform for presenting term papers, final papers, scientific essays, dissertations and specialist books.

Visit us on the internet:

http://www.grin.com/

http://www.facebook.com/grincom

http://www.twitter.com/grin_com

Table of Contents

CHAPTER 1: INTRODUCTION

1.1 Objective of the work

The main objective of this work is to use an estimator for imputing missing values in mixed attribute datasets by utilising the information present in incomplete instances also apart from the complete instances. This approach prevents loss of information which occurs when continuous values are converted into discrete values and vice versa for imputation.

This method is evaluated with extensive experiments and is compared with some typical algorithms and the performance is evaluated in terms of root mean square error and correlation coefficients.

This chapter begins with the brief introduction to data mining concepts, missing values and missing value imputation and concludes with the organization of the report.

1.2 Introduction to data mining

Data mining is the process of extraction of hidden predictive information from large databases. It is a powerful tool in by modern business to transform data into business intelligence giving an informational advantage. It is currently used in a wide range of profiling practices, such as marketing, surveillance, fraud detection, and scientific discovery. It can also be defined as the process of discovering interesting knowledge from large amount of data stored either in databases, data warehouses or other information repositories.

Data Mining is a step in the knowledge discovery process consisting of particular data mining algorithms. It is a powerful new technology with great potential to help companies focus on the most important information in their data warehouses. Data mining is primarily used today by companies with a stronger consumer focus retail, financial, communication and marketing organizations. It enables these companies to determine relationships among internal factors such as economic indicators, competition, and consumer demography and it enables them to determine the impact on sales, customer satisfaction , and corporate profits.

3

Data mining consists of five major elements:

- Extract, transform and load transaction data onto the data ware house system.
- Store and manage the data in a multidimensional database system.
- Provide data access to business analysts and information technology professionals.
- Analyze the data by application software.
- Present the data in a useful format , such as graph or a table.

Data mining techniques

Data mining is an in disciplinary field ,the confluence of a set of disciplines including database systems, statistics, machine learning, visualization and information science. Some commonly used data mining techniques are,

- **Artificial neural networks:** Non-Linear predictive models that learn through training and resemble biological neural networks in structure.
- **Decision trees:** Tree-shaped structures that represents sets of decisions. These decisions generate rules for the classification of a dataset. Specific decision tree methods include classification and Regression (CART) and Chi square Automated Integration Detection (CHAID).
- **Genetic Algorithms:** Optimization techniques that use process such as genetic combination, and natural selection in a design based on the concepts of evolution.
- **Nearest neighbor method:** A technique that classifies each record in a dataset based on a combination of the classes of the k record most similar to it in a historical dataset. Sometimes called the k-nearest neighbor technique.
- **Association rule induction:** The extraction of useful if-then rules from data based on statistical significance.

Many of these technologies have been in use for more than a decade in specialized analysis tool that work with relatively small volume s of data. These capabilities are now evolving to integrate directly with industry-standard data warehouse and OLAP platforms.

Data mining tasks

Data mining commonly involves four classes of tasks:

- **Clustering:** is the task of discovering groups and structures in the data that are in some way or another similar without using known structures in the data.
- **Classification:** is the task of generalizing structure to apply to new data. Common algorithms include decision tree learning, nearest neighbor, naive Bayesian classification, neural networks and support vector machines.
- **Regression:** Attempts to find a function which models the data with the least error.
- **Association rule learning:** Searches for relationship between variables.

1.3 Missing values

Many types of experimental data, especially expression data obtained from microarray experiments and air pollutant data obtained from air sample collecting machine are frequently peppered with Missing values (MVs) that may occur for a variety of reasons and they need to be preprocessed.

Tasks in data preprocessing are:

- **Data cleaning: fill in missing values**
- Data integration
- Data transformation: normalization and aggregation.
- Data reduction: reducing the volume but producing the same or similar analytical results.
- Data discretization

Because many data analyses such as classification methods, clustering methods and dimension reduction procedures require complete data, researchers must either remove the data with MVs, or, preferably, estimate the MVs before such procedures can be employed. Consequently, many algorithms have been developed to accurately impute MVs. Because missing values can result in bias that impacts on the quality of learned patterns or/and the performance of classifications, missing data imputation has been a key issue in learning from incomplete data. Many existing, industrial and research data sets contain Missing Values. They are introduced due to various reasons, such as manual data entry procedures, equipment errors

5

and incorrect measurements. The detection of incomplete data is not easy in most cases. Missing Values (MVs) can appear with the form of outliers or even wrong data (i.e. out of boundaries).

Three basic approaches to deal with missing values

- Case deletion.
- Learning without handling of missing values.
- **Missing value imputation.**

1.4 Missing value imputation

Missing value imputation is a procedure that replaces the missing values with some feasible values. Various techniques have been developed with great successes on dealing with missing values in data sets with homogeneous attributes (their independent attributes are all either continuous or discrete). However, these imputation algorithms cannot be applied to many real data sets, such as equipment maintenance databases, industrial data sets, and gene databases, because these data sets are often with both continuous and discrete independent attributes. These heterogeneous data sets are referred to as mixed-attribute data sets and their independent attributes are called as mixed independent attributes. Imputing mixed-attribute data sets can be taken as a new problem in missing data imputation because there is no estimator designed for imputing missing data in mixed attribute data sets. The challenging issues include, such as how to measure the relationship between instances (transactions) in a mixed-attribute data set, and how to construct hybrid estimators using the observed data in the data set.

6

1.5 Model flow diagram

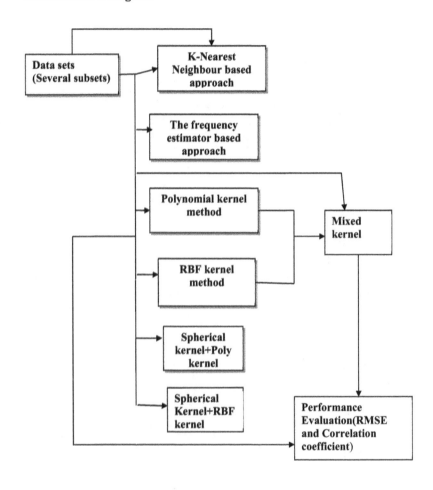

1.1 Data flow diagram(Author's own work)

Fig 1.1gives an overview of the work. The original data sets are subjected to pre processing techniques which here refers to creating missing values randomly and the missing values are imputed using K-NN, Frequency estimator method, RBF kernel and Polynomial kernel, a mixed kernel (RBF kernel and Poly kernel), and a spherical kernel mixed with poly kernel and a spherical kernel mixed with RBF kernel.

Finally, the performance of these imputation methods is evaluated using Root Mean Square Error(RMSE) and Correlation Coefficient.

1.6 Organizationof the report

The report is organized as follows,

Chapter 2 provides an overview of the literature review

Chapter 3 describes about the dataset description

Chapter 4 presents the implementation results

Chapter 5 presents Imputation using kernel functions

Chapter 6 presents results and discussion

Chapter 7 provides conclusion and future work

1.7 Summary

This chapter discussed about data mining, scope of data mining, various data mining methods, Missing values, Missing value imputation and Data flow diagram , thereby giving an overview about the basic concepts.

CHAPTER 2: LITERATURE REVIEW

2.1 Introduction

This chapter presents previous studies done in the field of missing values, missing value imputation techniques and kernel functions. It deals with the background studies in the field of missing values and gives an idea about the imputation methods carried out in this field.

2.2 Literature review

2.2.1 Missing values

Allison, P. D. (2001) in the paper, Missing data has evaluated two algorithms for producing multiple imputations or missing data using simulated data based on the software of SOLAS. Software using a propensity score classifier with the approximate Bayesian bootstrap was found to produce badly biased estimates of regression coefficients when data on predictor variables are MAR or MACR.

Brown, M. L., & Kros, J. F.,(2003) in the paper, Data Mining and Impact of missing data explained the importance of estimating missing data in datasets especially in the case of real data sets. Data mining is based upon searching the concatenation of multiple databases that usually contain some amount of missing data along with a variable percentage of inaccurate data, pollution, outliers, and noise. The actual data-mining process deals significantly with prediction, estimation, classification, pattern recognition, and the development of association rules. Therefore, the significance of the analysis depends heavily on the accuracy of the database and on the chosen sample data to be used for model training and testing. The issue of missing data must be addressed since ignoring this problem can introduce bias into the models being evaluated and lead to inaccurate data mining conclusions.

S.C. Zhang et al. (2004) in the paper, Information enhancement in data mining indicated the presence of missing values and pointed out the importance of information enhancement and data pre-processing in the raw data. Information enhancement techniques are desired in many areas such as data mining, machine learning, business intelligence, and web data analysis. Information enhancement mainly includes the following topics: data cleaning, data preparation and transformation, missing values imputation, feature and instance selection, feature construction, treatment of noisy and inconsistent data, data integration, data collection and housing, information enhancement, web data availability, web data capture and representation, and the others

Ghahramani, Z., & Jordan, M. I. (1997) in the paper, Mixture models for learning from incomplete data has reviewed the main missing data techniques, including conventional methods, global imputation, local imputation, parameter estimation and direct management of missing data. He tried to highlight the advantages and disadvantages for all kinds of missing data mechanisms. For example, he revealed that statistical methods have been mainly developed to manage survey data and proved to be very effective in many situations. However, the main problem of these techniques is its strong model assumptions.

Zhang, S et al.,(2005) in the paper Missing is useful , missing values in cost sensitive decision tree studied the issue of missing attribute values in training and test data sets. Indeed, many real-world data sets contain missing values and a difficult problem to cope with. Sometimes, values are missing due to unknown reasons or errors and omissions when data are recorded and transferred. However, deleting casescan result in the loss of a large amount of valuable data. In this paper, they study missing data in cost-sensitive learning in which both misclassification costs and test costs are considered. That is, there is a known cost associated with each attribute (variable or test) when obtaining its values.

Feng, D. C (2008)in the paper, Research on missing value estimation in data mining explained the advantage of MAR (missing at random) pattern which is introduced on the basis of the analysis of all the missing pattern and EM(expectation maximum) algorithm were applied in MAR pattern correspondingly. Finally, the missing estimation algorithm was used in the pre-treatment stage of fault data and combined with wavelet neural network to realize the fault classification. Mean value algorithm will easily cause the estimation error and reduce the association trend among the variables. However, the missing value estimation process may change the original information system more or less; even add the noise during the filling process of null value, which will probably cause the wrong results in data mining. Therefore, how to realize the data mining with null value directly rather than changing the original information system still need further research.

2.2.2 Missing value imputation

Qin, Y et al.(2007)in the paper, Semi parametric optimization for missing data imputation gave the idea that Missing data imputation is an important issue in machine learning and data mining. In this paper, a new and efficient imputation method for a kind of missing data: semi-parametric data is proposed. This imputation method aims at making an optimal evaluation about Root Mean Square Error (RMSE), distribution function and quintile after missing-data are imputed.

Zhang, C et al. (2007) in the paper, An imputation method for missing values gave an idea that it is necessary to iteratively impute missing values while suffering from large missing ratio. Hence, many iterative imputation methods have been developed, such as the Expectation-Maximization (EM) algorithm which is a classical parametric method.

Dick, U et al.(2008),in the paper ,Learning with incomplete data with infinite imputation addresses the problem of learning decision functions from training data in which some attribute values are unobserved. This problem can arise, for instance, when training data is aggregated sources, and some sources record only a subset of attributes. A generic joint optimization problem in which the distribution governing the missing values is a free parameter is derived. It is shown that the optimal solution concentrates the density mass on finitely many imputations, and provides a corresponding algorithm for learning from incomplete data.

Ling, W et al.(2009) in the paper , Estimation of missing values using a weighted K-Nearest Neighbors algorithm presented a novel algorithm that iscapable of simultaneously estimating several missing components using a weighted K-Nearest-Neighbors algorithm.. This paper studied a new imputation method towards the task of establishing a model from observation data when missing values occur among the multivariate input data. The main idea is to exploit correlations between different dimensions in Weighted-KNN distance metric when imputing the missing dimension, where each dimension should be weighted by the respective correlation coefficient obtained by the SVR method. The imputation method is stimulated by the steel corrosion dataset in seawater environmental, which was demonstrated to have superior results to the KNN imputation method.

11

2.2.3 Kernel functions

Silverman, B. W. (2018) in the paper , Density estimation for statistics and data analysis pointed out that the selection of optimal bandwidth is much more important than kernel function selection. This is because smaller values of bandwidth make the estimate look "wiggly" and show spurious characteristics, whereas too large values of bandwidth will result in an estimation that is too smooth, in the sense that it is too biased to reveal structural features. However, there is not a generally accepted method for choosing the optimal bandwidth.

Racine, J., & Li, Q. (2004) in the paper, Non- parametric estimation of regression functions with both categorical and continuous data proposed a method for nonparametric regression which admits continuous and categorical data in a natural manner using the method of kernels. A data-driven method of bandwidth selection is proposed, and the asymptotic normality of the estimator is established. The rate of convergence of the cross-validated smoothing parameters to their benchmark optimal smoothing parameters was also established.

Smits, G. F., & Jordaan, E. M. (2002) in the paper, Improved SVM regression using mixture of kernelsexplained that a mixed kernel, a linear combination between poly kernel and Gaussian kernel, gives the extrapolation and interpolation much better than either a local kernel or a global kernel. In this paper, a mixture of kernels is employed to replace the single kernel in continuous kernel estimator.

Raykar, V. C., & Duraiswami, R. (2006) in the paper, Fast optimal bandwidth selection for kernel density estimation proposed a computationally approximation algorithm for univariate Gaussian kernel based density derivative estimation that reduces the computational complexity from $O(MN)$ to linear $O(N+M)$. The procedure is applied to estimate the optimal bandwidth for kernel density estimation. The speedup achieved on this problem is demonstrated using the "solve-the-equation plug-in" method, and on exploratory projection pursuit techniques.

Xiaofeng Zhu et al.(2011)in the paper ,Missing value estimation in mixed attribute data sets explained a new setting of missing data imputation, i.e., imputing missing data in data sets with heterogeneous attributes (their independent attributes are of different types), referred to as imputing mixed-attribute data sets. This paper first proposes two consistent estimators for discrete and continuous missing target values, respectively. And then, a mixture-kernel based iterative estimator is advocated to impute mixed-attribute data sets .

2.3 Summary

This chapter gives a detailed view about the work done by authors in the field of missing value, missing value imputation and the use of kernel functions for imputation which are considered in this work.

CHAPTER 3: DATASET DESCRIPTION

3.1 Introduction

Missing value imputation is a key issue in learning from incomplete data. Various techniques have been developed to deal with missing values in data sets having homogenous attributes. However, these techniques cannot be applied to real data sets as these data sets such as such as equipment maintenance databases, industrial data sets, and gene databases, because these data sets are often with both continuous and discrete independent attributes. Hence a new set of imputation has been developed to impute missing data in mixed attribute data sets.

This chapter gives a brief introduction about the datasets used in the experiments and the number of attributes and instances in these data sets.

3.2 Data set description

Five publicly available data sets are used in this work namely Auto-mpg, Housing, Abalone , Pima and Vowel. These data sets are obtained from UCI machine learning repository and these data sets does not contain any missing values. The missing values are created at random in these datasets and are imputed using the techniques used in this work. Finally the performance of these techniques is evaluated using root mean square error and correlation coefficient.

The data sets used in the experiments are mainly obtained from UCI machine learning data repository. Table 3.1 gives details about the datasets used in this work.

Name	Type	#(attr.)	#(ins.)
Auto-mpg	Mixed	8	398
Housing	Mixed	14	506
Abalone	Mixed	8	4177
Pima	Mixed	8	768
Vowel	Mixed	10	528

Table 3.1 Datasets used in the experiments

In the above table 3.1, the first column indicates the name of the data sets used, the second column denoting type and the third column indicates the number of the attributes and the last column denotes the number of instances in these data sets. A mixture kernel based iterative

14

estimator using spherical kernel and RBF and Poly kernels are used to impute the missing values in these data sets.

3.3 Summary

This chapter discussed about the data sets used in the work. Missing value imputation eliminates the problem of bias caused by the presence of missing values in the real data sets. These data sets are used to evaluate the performance of the techniques used in this work.

CHAPTER 4: IMPUTATION TECHNIQUES

4.1 Introduction

This chapter gives a detailed view about the imputation techniques used in the work namely K-Nearest neighbor, Frequency estimator technique, Imputation using RBF kernel, and Imputation using Poly kernel.

4.2 K –Nearest neighbor imputation method

Missing data imputation is an important step in the process of machine learning and data mining when certain values are missed. Among extant imputation techniques, kNN imputation algorithm is the best one as it is a model free and efficient compared with other methods. However, the value of k must be chosen properly in using kNN imputation.

This subsection deals with the K-Nearest neighbor imputation methods which is explained as follows.

1. Determine parameter K = number of nearest neighbors

2. Calculate the distance between the query-instance and all the training samples

3. Sort the distance and determine nearest neighbors based on the K-th minimum distance

4. Gather the values of Y of the nearest neighbors

5. Use average of nearest neighbors as the prediction value of the query instance

4.3 Experimental results for imputation done using K-NN

Table 4.1 shows the experimental results for K-NN.

Data set	RMSE(%)	Correlation coefficient(%)
Auto-import	0.84791	0.650316
Housing	0.83133	0.67677
Abalone	0.82891	0.66499
Pima	0.83113	0.66962
Vowel	0.83501	0.67313

Table 4.1 Experimental results for K-NN

4.4 Frequency Estimation Method

The probability density function of each instance in the row is calculated and the value which is having the highest probability density function is replaced in place of the missing value. This method is good for discrete datasets.

4.5 Experimental results for frequency estimator

Data set	RMSE(%)	Correlation coefficient(%)
Auto-import	0.84791	0.650316
Housing	0.83133	0.67677
Abalone	0.82891	0.66499
Pima	0.83113	0.66962
Vowel	0.83501	0.67313

Table 4.2 Experimental results for Frequency estimator

From the table 4.2 the experimental results of frequency estimator indicates that it imputes missing values in a better way when compared to K-NN method.

4.6 Kernel Functions

Kernels are used in Support Vector Machines to map the learning data (nonlinearly) into a higher dimensional feature space where the computational power of the linear learning machine is increased. The level of non-linearity is determined by the kernel function. There are two main types of kernels, namely Local and Global kernels. In local kernels only the data that are close or in the proximity of each other have an influence on the kernel values. In contrast, a global kernel allows data points that are far away from each other to have an influence on the kernel values as well. In this work polynomial and RBF kernels are chosen The Polynomial and RBF kernels are used again for the analysis of the interpolation and extrapolation abilities. The reason for analyzing these two types of kernels is twofold. Firstly, they can be used as representatives of a broader class of local and global kernels respectively. Secondly, these kernels have computational advantages over other kernels, since it is easier and faster to compute the kernel.

4.7 Imputation using RBF kernel

An example of a typical local kernel is the Radial Basis Function Kernel (RBF), which is defined in equ(1) as follows,

$$K(x,x_i)=\exp(- \mid x-x_i \mid ^2)/2\sigma^2 \qquad (1)$$

where the kernel parameter is the width, σ, of the radial basis function. A local kernel only has an effect on the data points in the neighbourhood of the test point. In Figure 4.1 the local effect of the RBF Kernel is shown for a chosen test input, for different values of the width σ .

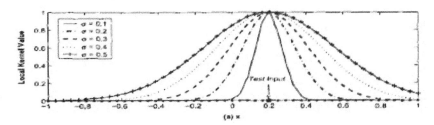

Fig 4.1 Local effect of RBF kernel (Smits, G. F., & Jordaan, E. M. 2002)

17

The missing values are imputed using RBF kernel by choosing a value fpr kernel width σ for which the root mean square error is minimum and correlation coefficient is maximum[34].

4.8 Experimental results for rbf kernel

Data set	RMSE(%)	Correlation coefficient(%)
Auto-import	0.67391	0.79169
Housing	0.67604	0.78596
Abalone	0.66456	0.78271
Pima	0.69127	0.80854
Vowel	0.65332	0.81460

Table 4.3 Experimental results for RBF kernel

From the table 4.3 the experimental results of RBF kernel indicates that it imputes missing values in a better way when compared to the previous methods discussed above .

4.9 Imputation using poly kernel

The polynomial kernel is a typical example of global kernel which is defined in equ (2) as follows

$$K(x,x_i)=[(x-x_i)+1]^q \qquad (2)$$

where the kernel parameter q is the degree of polynomial to be used. A global kernel allows data points that are far away from each other to have an influence on the kernel values as well. In Figure 4.,2 the global effect of the Polynomial kernel of various degrees is shown.

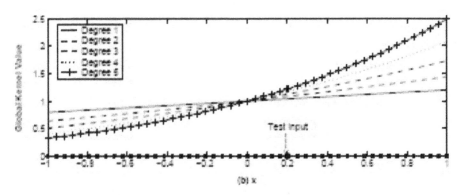

Fig 4.2 Global kernel (Smits, G. F., & Jordaan, E. M. 2002)

For each degree of polynomial, all data points in the input domain have non-zero kernel values. The test data point has a global effect on the other data points. The missing values are imputed using a degree of polynomial 2 to get minimum value of root mean square error and maximum value of correlation coefficient.

4.10 Experimental results for poly kernel

Data set	RMSE(%)	Correlation coefficient(%)
Auto-import	0.73081	0.74300
Housing	0.76276	0.73970
Abalone	0.73970	0.73512
Pima	0.79836	0.73336
Vowel	0.74872	0.74872

Table 4.4 Experimental results for Poly kernel

From the table 4.4 the experimental results of Poly kernel indicates that it imputes missing values in a better way when compared to the previous methods discussed above .

19

4.11 Summary

This chapter discussed about the different techniques used for imputation in this work thereby providing an overall idea about the different imputation techniques used. The frequency estimator technique discussed above works better for discrete attributes whereas in the case of RBF kernels , the kernel width should be properly chosen for exhibiting better interpolation and extrapolation abilities. Similarly, the degree of Polynomial should be chosen against interpolation and extrapolation abilities.

CHAPTER 5: IMPUTATION USING MIXTURE OF KERNELS

5.1 Introduction

This chapter deals with the possibility of using mixture of kernel functions for imputation namely mixing of RBF kernel and Poly kernel and also gives an idea about the mixing of higher order kernel functions like spherical kernel with an RBF kernel and spherical kernel with a Poly kernel for imputing missing data. The mixture of kernel functions when used exhibit better interpolation and extrapolation abilities.

5.2 Interpolation and Extrapolation

The quality of a model is not only determined by its ability to learn from the data but also its ability to predict unseen data. These two characteristics are often called learning capacity and generalization ability. Models are seldom good in both of the two characteristics. A typical example is the interpolation and extrapolation abilities of a model. These characteristics are largely determined by the choice of kernel and kernel parameters. Using a specific type of kernel has its advantages and disadvantages. The Polynomial and RBF kernels are used again for the analysis of the interpolation and extrapolation abilities. The reason for analyzing these two types of kernels is twofold. Firstly, they can be used as representatives of a broader class of local and global kernels respectively. Secondly, these kernels have computational advantages over other kernels, since it is easier and faster to compute the kernel values.

However, it is observed that that for lower degrees of polynomial kernels the extrapolation ability gets better. However, for good interpolation ability higher degree polynomials are required, No single choice of kernel parameter, the degree of the polynomial, results in an estimator for imputation that will provide both good interpolation and extrapolation properties. Similarly, in RBF kernel if large values of σ are used the interpolation ability of RBF Kernels decreases. Therefore, no single value of the kernel parameter, σ, will provide an estimator with both good interpolation and extrapolation properties.

5.3 Mixture of kernels

From the previous section, it is observed that a polynomial kernel (a global kernel) shows better extrapolation abilities at lower orders of the degrees, but requires higher orders of degrees for good interpolation. On the other hand, the RBF kernel (a local

kernel) has good interpolation abilities, but fails to provide longer range extrapolation. Therefore, a mixture of kernel functions namely, RBF kernel and Polynomial kernel can be used for constructing an estimator for imputing the missing values.

There are several ways of mixing kernels, it is important that the resulting kernel must be an admissible kernel. One way to guarantee that the mixed kernel is admissible, is to use a convex combination of the two kernels Kpoly and Krbf, for example, the mixing of the two kernels is done in the following way as given in equ (3). It has been proved experimentally that only a "pinch" of a local kernel, (i.e., 1- ρ = 0.01), needs to be added to the global kernel in order to obtain a combination of good interpolation and extrapolation abilities.

$$K_{mix} = \rho K_{poly} + (1 - \rho K_{rbf}) \qquad (3)$$

where the optimal mixing coefficient ρ has to be determined. The value of ρ is a constant scalar.

In the experiments, the coefficients, ρ, q, and σ are combined with the coefficient λ so as to optimize the Approximate Mean Integrated Square Error(AMISE). First, the value of ρ is limited. If the data are in a (0, 1) scaled input space, a pure RBF-kernel with ρ> 0:4 behaves like a lower degree polynomial in the known learning space.

The RBF-kernel part is specifically needed when modelling the local behaviour. On

21

the other hand, using one λ that is too small will result in overly complex models that also model the noise. Therefore, it is appropriate that λ be set between 0.15 and 0.3 in this approach. Second, as a global kernel, the polynomial kernel is very good at capturing general trends and extrapolation behaviour. The extrapolation behaviour of

the model becomes erratic and shows sudden increases or decreases in the response surface when the value of q is too high. So, a lower degree for the polynomial kernel may be chosen. In the experiments, d > 2 is seldom used, and q is usually set to 1 or 2. Third, the choice of ρ is related to how much of the local behaviour needs to be modelled by the RBF kernel. Since the RBF-kernel is a very powerful kernel for

modelling local behaviour, it will not need much of its effects in order to see a huge improvement in the model. In the experiments, it is better if to choose the value of ρ between 0.95 and 0.99.

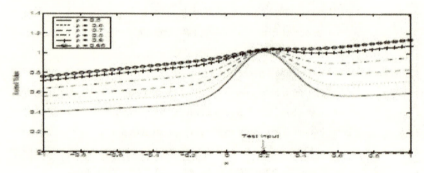

Fig5.3 Example of a mixed kernel(Smits, G. F., & Jordaan, E. M. 2002)

Figure 5.3, shows the effect of mixing a Polynomial kernel with a RBF Kernel .

Two consistent kernel functions one for discrete and one for continuous are designed and the two functions are combined to design a mixture kernel function for imputation which is defined in equ (4) as follows.

$$K_{h,\lambda,\ ix} = K(^{x-}x_{ih})\ L(X_{id,}\ x_{id},\ \lambda) \qquad\qquad (4)$$

where h → 0 and λ → 0 (λ; h is the smoothing parameter for the discrete and continuous kernel functions, respectively), and $K_{h;\lambda;ix}$ is a symmetric probability density function. Using the above function, the missing values are imputed for the datasets Abalone, Housing, Import, Pima and Vowel and the performance is evaluated using root mean square error and correlation coefficient.

5.4 Experimental results for mixture of kernels

Data set	RMSE(%)	Correlation coefficient(%)
Auto-import	0.653771	0.828723
Housing	0.65959	0.840341
Abalone	0.626433	0.837200
Pima	0.640855	0.844440
Vowel	0.637210	0.855701

Table 5.1 Experimental results for mixture of kernels

Fig 5.1 shows the experimental results for mixture of kernel. From the above results it is clear that mixture of kernel functions imputes better than the previous techniques like K-NN, frequency estimator, rbf kernel, poly kernel.

5.5 Imputation using spherical kernel with rbf kernel

In this technique the imputation of missing values is done using a mixture of higher order kernel function namely spherical kernel and RBF kernel and also spherical kernel with a polynomial kernel. The spherical kernel is a higher order kernel which has higher rate of computation and it is defined in equ (5)as follows

$$K(x, x_i) = 1 - 3/2 \| x - x_i \| / \sigma + \frac{1}{2} (\| x - x_i \| / \sigma) 3 \tag{5}$$

The mixing of spherical kernel with RBF kernel is done in the following way and the new kernel function is defined in equ (6) as follows

$$K_{mix} = \rho K_{sph} + (1 - \rho K_{rbf}) \tag{6}$$

In this method the value of ρ is a constant scalar and analysis should be done to find the best combination of the values λ, σ, q and d. The best result can be obtained by scanning all the combinations of σ, q, λ, and d, where the complexity is reduced compared with the original one due to the limited search space.

23

5.6 Experimental results for imputation using spherical kernel and rbf kernel

Data set	RMSE(%)	Correlation coefficient(%)
Auto-import	0.60339	0.90026
Housing	0.54889	0.94115
Abalone	0.59907	0.90098
Pima	0.59330	0.90928
Vowel	0.58710	0.90864

Table 5.2 Experimental results for mixture of kernels

Fig 5.2 shows the experimental results for imputation using spherical kernel and rbf kernel. From the above results it is clear that spherical kernel and rbf kernel imputes better than the previous techniques like K-NN, frequency estimator , rbf kernel, poly kernel and mixture of kernels in terms of rmse and correlation coefficient.

5.7 Imputation using spherical kernel and poly kernel

As described in the previous section, the imputation is also done using a mixture of spherical kernel and Poly kernel which is defined in equ (7) as follows

$$K_{mix} = \rho\, K_{sph} + (1 - \rho\, K_{poly}) \qquad\qquad (7)$$

Using the above kernel function an estimator is created for imputation of missing values and the performance is evaluated for all the techniques mentioned above, with respect to root mean square error and correlation coefficient.

5.8 Experimental results for spherical kernel and poly kernel

Data set	RMSE(%)	Correlation coefficient(%)
Auto-import	0.564306	0.93987
Housing	0.54889	0.92622
Abalone	0.59907	0.91465
Pima	0.59330	0.94723
Vowel	0.58710	0.93715

Table 5.3 Experimental results for mixture of kernels

Fig 5.3 shows the experimental results for imputation using spherical kernel and Poly kernel. From the above results it is clear that spherical kernel and poly kernel imputes better than the previous techniques like K-NN, frequency estimator , rbf kernel, poly kernel and mixture of kernels in terms of rmse and correlation coefficient.

5.9 Summary

This chapter discussed about the imputation of missing values done using mixture of kernels namely RBF and Poly kernels and also how it can be extended and implemented using mixture of spherical kernel and RBF kernel and also using spherical kernel with Poly kernel. It dealt with the extrapolation and interpolation abilities and how the kernel width, degree of Polynomial should be chosen for better extrapolation and interpolation abilities.

CHAPTER 6: RESULTS AND DISCUSSION

6.1 Introduction

This chapter deals with the performance evaluation and describes about the metrics used for evaluating the performance of the techniques used in this work. The performance is evaluated against root mean square error and correlation coefficient. The root mean square error and correlation coefficient are calculated for all the five data sets namely Abalone, Import, Housing, Vowel and Pima and results are compared.

6.2 Performance evaluation

The performance is evaluated using Root mean square error (RMSE) and correlation coefficient.

The RMSE is used to assess the predictive ability after the algorithm has converged. It is calculated as given in equ (8)

$$RMSE= \sqrt{1/m}\sum_{i=1}^{m}(e_i - \sim e_i)^2 \qquad (8)$$

where e_i is the original attribute value; $\sim e_i$ is the estimated attribute value, and m is the total number of predictions. The larger the value of the RMSE, the less accurate the prediction is.
The correlation coefficient(cc) is usually defined as follows as given in equ(9)

$$CC= \frac{\sum xy - \sum x \sum y)}{\sqrt{([n\sum x^2-(\sum x)^2] [n(\sum y^2-(\sum y)^2)}} \qquad (9)$$

Where x denotes the original value, y denotes the imputed value and n denotes the number of counts.

6.3 Experimental results and discussion

The root mean square error and correlation coefficient are calculated for all the techniques discussed and the performance is compared. The RMSE value and correlation coefficient are calculated for all the datasets as discussed above. Table 6.1 to Table 6.5 gives the results of RMSE and correlation coefficient for Auto-Import, Housing, Abalone, Pima and Vowel data set. It can be observed from these tables that the imputation done using spherical kernel works better when compared to the other methods as the root mean square error is minimum and correlation coefficient is maximum when missing values are imputed using spherical kernel with RBF and spherical kernel with poly kernel.

S.NO	Technique used	Performance evaluation	
		RMSE(%)	Correlation coefficient(%)
1	K-NN	0.847193	0.650316
2	Frequency estimator	0.809691	0.719151
3	RBF kernel	0.673918	0.791693
4	Poly kernel	0.730813	0.743009
5	Mixed kernel(RBF and Poly)	0.653771	0.828723
6	Spherical and RBF	0.603390	0.900268
7	Spherical and Poly	0.564306	0.939870

Table 6.1 RMSE and correlation coefficient for Auto-Import data set

S.NO	Technique used	Performance evaluation	
		RMSE(%)	Correlation coefficient(%)
1	K-NN	0.83133	0.67677
2	Frequency estimator	0.80052	0.68361
3	RBF kernel	0.67604	0.78596
4	Poly kernel	0.76276	0.73970
5	Mixed kernel(RBF and Poly)	0.65959	0.84034
6	Spherical and RBF	0.54589	0.94115
7	Spherical and Poly	0.57777	0.92622

Table 6.2 RMSE and correlation coefficient for Housing data set

In the case of Housing data set it can be noted that the imputation done using higher order kernel that is spherical kernel works better when compared to the other techniques.

S.NO	Technique used	Performance evaluation	
		RMSE(%)	Correlation coefficient(%)
1	K-NN	0.828916	0.664992
2	Frequency estimator	0.797110	0.68188
3	RBF kernel	0.664569	0.78271
4	Poly kernel	0.739704	0.73512
5	Mixed kernel(RBF and Poly)	0.626433	0.83720
6	Spherical and RBF	0.599079	0.90098
7	Spherical and Poly	0.561547	0.91465

Table 6.3 RMSE and correlation coefficient for Abalone data set

S.NO	Technique used	Performance evaluation	
		RMSE(%)	Correlation coefficient(%)
1	K-NN	0.831138	0.66962
2	Frequency estimator	0.806693	0.71810
3	RBF kernel	0.699127	0.80854
4	Poly kernel	0.748365	0.73336
5	Mixed kernel(RBF and Poly)	0.640833	0.84440
6	Spherical and RBF	0.593330	0.90928
7	Spherical and Poly	0.553242	0.94723

Table 6.4 RMSE and correlation coefficient for Pima data set

S.NO	Technique used	Performance evaluation	
		RMSE(%)	Correlation coefficient(%)
1	K-NN	0.83501	0.67313
2	Frequency estimator	0.80778	0.71755
3	RBF kernel	0.65332	0.81460
4	Poly kernel	0.74872	0.74872
5	Mixed kernel(RBF and Poly)	0.63721	0.81570
6	Spherical and RBF	0.58710	0.90864
7	Spherical and Poly	0.52089	0.93715

Table 6.5 RMSE and correlation coefficient for Vowel data set

6.4 Discussion of results

From the above results it is observed that spherical kernel which is a higher order kernel when mixed with rbf kernel and Poly kernel gives a least value of rmse for all the data sets. It is also observed that correlation coefficient is maximum when imputation is done using spherical kernel with rbf and spherical kernel with poly Kernel. Thus it is observed that spherical kernel when mixed with rbf kernel and spherical kernel when mixed with Poly kernel produces better results. The performance graph for Root Mean square error is as shown for the data set Pima is as shown in fig 6.1

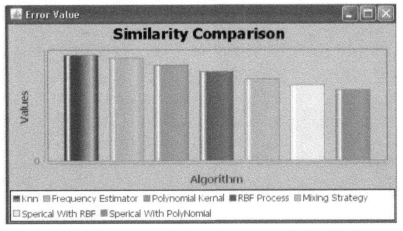

Fig 6.1 Performance comparison for root mean square error for Pima data set.

(Authors own work)

29

From the above fig 6.1,it is clear that imputation done using spherical kernel with RBF and spherical kernel with Poly kernel produces least value of Root mean square error when compared to the other techniques.

The performance evaluation for correlation coefficient for Pima data set is as shown in fig 6.2

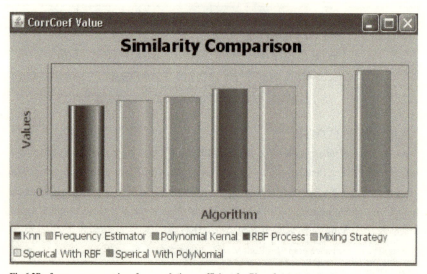

Fig 6.2Performance comparison for correlation coefficient for Pima data set.(Author's own work)

From the above fig 6.2 it is clear that imputation done using spherical kernel with RBF and spherical kernel with Poly kernel produces maximum value of correlation coefficient when compared to the other techniques.

6.5 Summary

This chapter discussed about the performance evaluation metrics and also gave an idea about the root mean square error and correlation coefficient for all the techniques used here. From the above results it is observed that spherical kernel when mixed with rbf and Poly kernels produce better results than other methods.

CHAPTER 7: CONCLUSION AND FUTURE WORK

7.1 Conclusion

In this work, a mixture kernel estimator using spherical kernel and Rbf kernel and also using spherical kernel and Poly kernel has been proposed for imputing missing values in a mixed-attribute data set. This mixture kernel-based iterative nonparametric estimator is proposed against the case that data sets have both continuous and discrete independent attributes. It utilizes all available observed information, including observed information in incomplete instances (with missing values), to impute missing values, whereas existing imputation methods use only the observed information in complete instances (without missing values). The optimal bandwidth is experimentally selected by a grid search method.

In this work missing values are imputed using seven techniques namely K-nearest neighbor, Frequency estimator, Poly kernel, RBF kernel, Mixture of Poly and RBF kernel, spherical kernel with RBF kernel, and spherical kernel with poly kernel and the performance of all these methods is evaluated using root mean square error and correlation coefficient.

7.2 Future work

The future work is to plan to further explore other kernel functions, instead of the existing ones, in order to achieve better extrapolation and interpolation abilities in learning algorithms. Other higher order kernel functions can be explored in the future to produce better results.

REFERENCES

[1] Allison, P. D. (2001). Missing data (quantitative applications in the social sciences).

[2] Brown, M. L., & Kros, J. F. (2003). Data mining and the impact of missing data. Industrial Management & Data Systems, 103(8), 611-621.

[3] Dick, U., Haider, P., & Scheffer, T. (2008, July). Learning from incomplete data with infinite imputations. In Proceedings of the 25th international conference on Machine learning (pp. 232-239). ACM.

[4] Feng, D. C., Wang, Z., Shi, J. F., & Pereira, J. D. (2008, June). Research on missing value estimation in data mining. In *2008 7th World Congress on Intelligent Control and Automation* (pp. 2048-2052). IEEE

[5] Ghahramani, Z., & Jordan, M. I. (1997). Mixture models for learning from incomplete data. Computational learning theory and natural learning systems, 4, 67-85.

[6] Racine, J., & Li, Q. (2004). Nonparametric estimation of regression functions with both categorical and continuous data. Journal of Econometrics, 119(1), 99-130

[7] Raykar, V. C., & Duraiswami, R. (2006, April). Fast optimal bandwidth selection for kernel density estimation. In *Proceedings of the 2006 SIAM International Conference on Data Mining* (pp. 524-528). Society for Industrial and Applied Mathematics

[8] Silverman, B. W. (2018). Density estimation for statistics and data analysis. Routledge

[9] Smits, G. F., & Jordaan, E. M. (2002). Improved SVM regression using mixtures of kernels. In Proceedings of the 2002 International Joint Conference on Neural Networks. IJCNN'02 (Cat. No. 02CH37290) (Vol. 3, pp. 2785-2790). IEEE.

[10] Qin, Y., Zhang, S., Zhu, X., Zhang, J., & Zhang, C. (2007). Semi-parametric optimization for missing data imputation. Applied Intelligence, 27(1), 79-88..

[11] Zhang, S., Qin, Z., Ling, C. X., & Sheng, S. (2005). " Missing is useful": missing values in cost-sensitive decision trees. *IEEE transactions on knowledge and data engineering, 17*(12), 1689-1693

[12] S.C. Zhang et al., "Information Enhancement for Data Mining,"IEEE Intelligent Systems, vol. 19, no. 2, pp. 12-13, Mar./Apr. 2004.

[13] Zhang, C., Zhu, X., Zhang, J., Qin, Y., & Zhang, S. (2007, May). GBKII: An imputation method for missing values. In *Pacific-Asia Conference on Knowledge Discovery and Data Mining* (pp. 1080-1087). Springer, Berlin, Heidelb

[14]   Ling, W., & Dong-Mei, F. (2009, July). Estimation of missing values using a
weighted k-nearest neighbors algorithm. In *2009 International Conference on
Environmental Science and Information Application Technology* (Vol. 3, pp. 660-663).
IEEE

[15]   Xiaofeng Zhu, Shichao Zhang, Zhi <u>Lin</u>, Zili Zhang, and Zhuoming Xu "Missing
value estimation in mixed attribute data sets" IEEE transactions on knowledge and data
engineering, vol. 23, no. 1, 2011

APPENDIX-A

SCREEN SHOTS

A.1 SELECTING A DATA SET

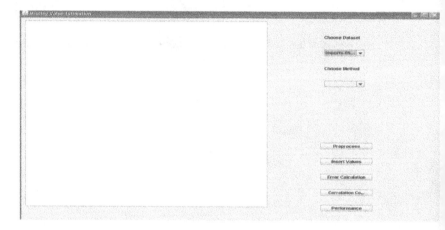

A.2 CHOOSING A TECHNIQUE

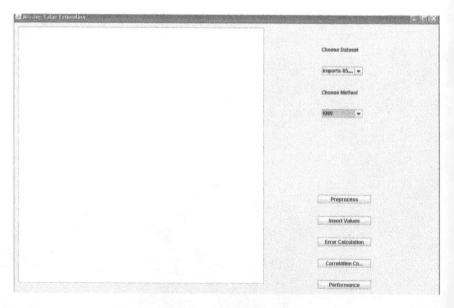

A.3 PREPROCESSING THE INPUT

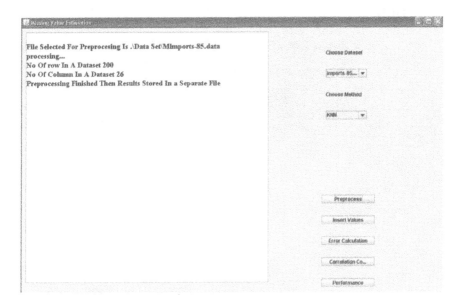

A.4 INSERTING VALUES BY USING K-NN METHOD

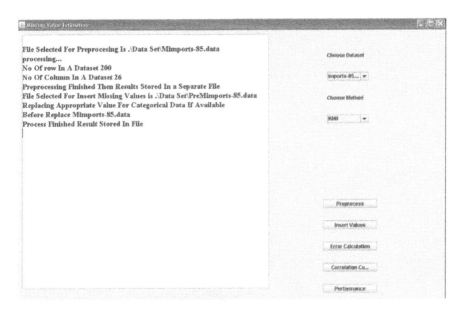

A.5 ROOT MEAN SQUARE ERROR CALCULATION FOR K-NN METHOD

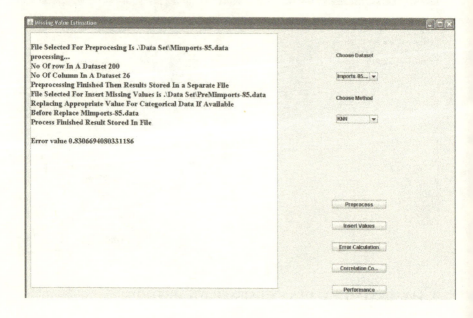

File Selected For Preprocesing Is .\Data Set\Mimports-85.data
processing...
No Of row In A Dataset 200
No Of Column In A Dataset 26
Preprocessing Finished Then Results Stored In a Separate File
File Selected For Insert Missing Values is .\Data Set\PreMimports-85.data
Replacing Appropriate Value For Categorical Data If Available
Before Replace Mimports-85.data
Process Finished Result Stored In File

Error value 0.8306694080331186

Choose Dataset

imports-85.... ▼

Choose Method

KNN ▼

Preprocess

Insert Values

Error Calculation

Correlation Co...

Performance

A.6 CALCULATION OF CORRELATION COEFFICIENT FOR K-NN METHOD

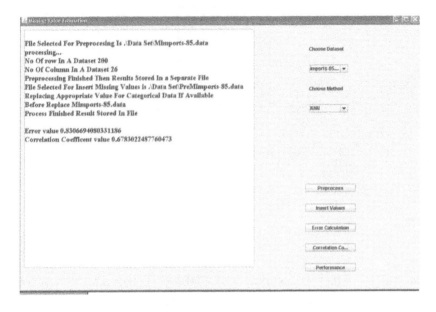

A.7 CALCULATION OF RMSE AND CORRELATION COEFFICIENT FOR FREQUENCY ESTIMATOR METHOD

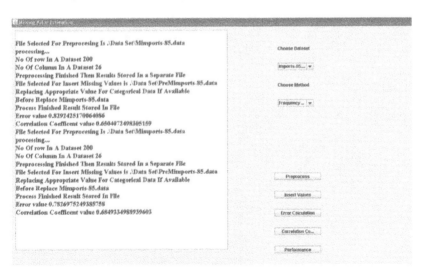

A.8 CALCULATION OF RMSE AND CORRELATION COEFFICIENT FOR POLYNOMIAL KERNEL METHOD

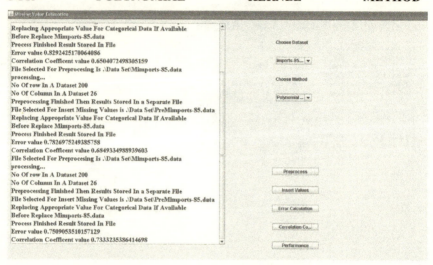

Missing Value Estimation

```
Replacing Appropriate Value For Categorical Data If Available
Before Replace Mimports-85.data
Process Finished Result Stored In File
Error value 0.8292425170064086
Correlation Coefficent value 0.6504072498305159
File Selected For Preprocesing Is .\Data Set\Mimports-85.data
processing...
No Of row In A Dataset 200
No Of Column In A Dataset 26
Preprocessing Finished Then Results Stored In a Separate File
File Selected For Insert Missing Values is .\Data Set\PreMimports-85.data
Replacing Appropriate Value For Categorical Data If Available
Before Replace Mimports-85.data
Process Finished Result Stored In File
Error value 0.7826975249385758
Correlation Coefficent value 0.6849334988939603
File Selected For Preprocesing Is .\Data Set\Mimports-85.data
processing...
No Of row In A Dataset 200
No Of Column In A Dataset 26
Preprocessing Finished Then Results Stored In a Separate File
File Selected For Insert Missing Values is .\Data Set\PreMimports-85.data
Replacing Appropriate Value For Categorical Data If Available
Before Replace Mimports-85.data
Process Finished Result Stored In File
Error value 0.7509053510157129
Correlation Coefficent value 0.7333235386414698
```

Choose Dataset

imports-85... ▼

Choose Method

Polynomial ... ▼

Preprocess

Insert Values

Error Calculation

Correlation Co...

Performance

A.9 CALCULATION OF RMSE AND CORRELATION COEFFICIENT FOR RBF KERNEL METHOD

Missing Value Estimation

```
Replacing Appropriate Value For Categorical Data If Available
Before Replace Mimports-85.data
Process Finished Result Stored In File
Error value 0.7826975249385758
Correlation Coefficent value 0.6849334988939603
File Selected For Preprocesing Is .\Data Set\Mimports-85.data
processing...
No Of row In A Dataset 200
No Of Column In A Dataset 26
Preprocessing Finished Then Results Stored In a Separate File
File Selected For Insert Missing Values is .\Data Set\PreMimports-85.data
Replacing Appropriate Value For Categorical Data If Available
Before Replace Mimports-85.data
Process Finished Result Stored In File
Error value 0.7509053510157129
Correlation Coefficent value 0.7333235386414698
File Selected For Preprocesing Is .\Data Set\Mimports-85.data
processing...
No Of row In A Dataset 200
No Of Column In A Dataset 26
Preprocessing Finished Then Results Stored In a Separate File
File Selected For Insert Missing Values is .\Data Set\PreMimports-85.data
Replacing Appropriate Value For Categorical Data If Available
Before Replace Mimports-85.data
Process Finished Result Stored In File
Error value 0.6709513514031061
Correlation Coefficent value 0.7815009820242609
```

Choose Dataset

imports-85... ▼

Choose Method

RBF Process ▼

Preprocess

Insert Values

Error Calculation

Correlation Co...

Performance

A.10 CALCULATION OF RMSE AND CORRELATION COEFFICIENT FOR MIXED STRATEGY

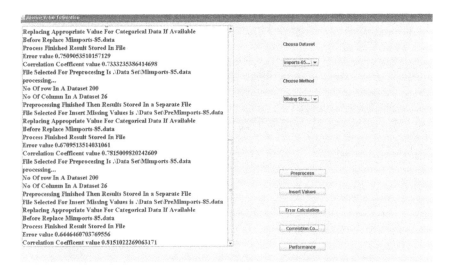

A.11 CALCULATION OF RMSE AND CORRELATION COEFFICIENT FOR SPHERICAL KERNEL WITH RBF KERNEL

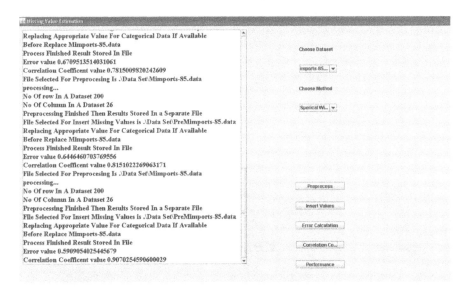

A.12 CALCULATION OF RMSE AND CORRELATION COEFFICIENT FOR SPHERICAL KERNEL WITH RBF KERNEL

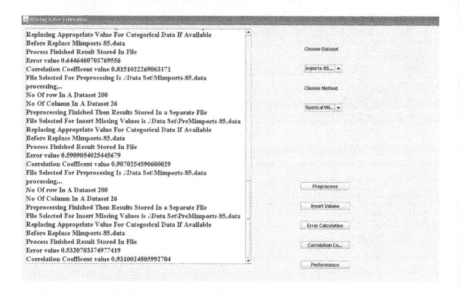

A.13 PERFOMANCE EVALUATION

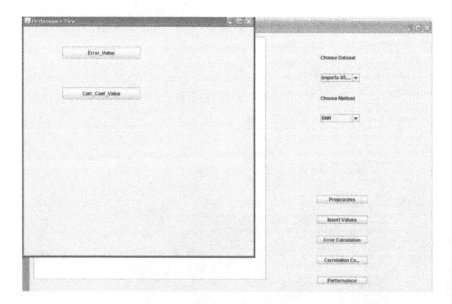

A.14 PERFOMANCE EVALUATION FOR RMSE

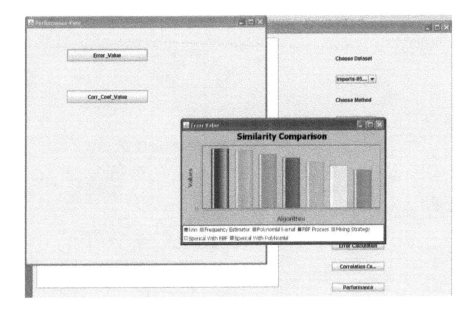

A.15 PERFOMANCE EVALATION FOR CORRELATION COEFFICIENT

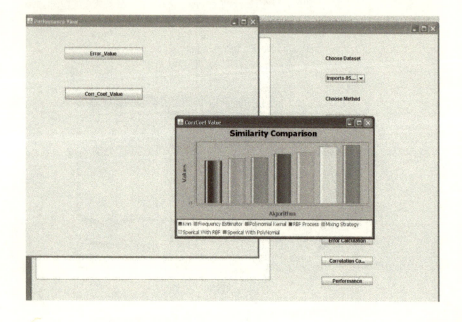

APPENDIX-B

LIST OF ABBREVIATIONS

K-NN K nearest neighbor

RBF   Radial basis function

RMSE   Root mean square error

PDF   Probability density function

Poly   Polynomial

www.ingramcontent.com/pod-product-compliance
Lightning Source LLC
LaVergne TN
LVHW042302060326
832902LV00009B/1205